Nature's Children

SALMON

Elma Schemenauer

 Grolier

FACTS IN BRIEF

Classification of Salmon

Class: *Actinopterygii* (ray-finned fish)

Order: *Salmoniformes* (salmon-shaped fish)

Family: *Salmonidae* (salmon family)

Genus: *Salmo*—Atlantic Salmon

Oncorhynchus—Pacific Salmon

Species: *Salmo salar* (Atlantic Salmon); 6 species of Pacific Salmon, 5 of which are found in North American waters: chinook, chum, coho, pink, sockeye.

World distribution. North Pacific and North Atlantic oceans and rivers emptying into them.

Habitat. Born in freshwater streams, salmon migrate to the ocean at different ages depending on species.

Distinctive physical characteristics. Species vary widely in size, color and markings, but all have pink flesh; size range 1-55 kilograms (2-120 pounds).

Habits. Major migration from sea to home streams for spawning.

Published originally as
"Getting to Know . . . Nature's Children."

This series is approved and recommended by the Federation of Ontario Naturalists.

Canadian Cataloguing in Publication Data

Schemenauer, Elma.
    Salmon

(Getting to know—nature's children)
Includes index.
ISBN 0-7172-1917-8

1. Salmon—Juvenile literature.
I. Title. II. Series.

QL638.S2S33 1985   j597'.55   C85-098734-2

Contents

Have you ever watched a fish in a fishbowl or aquarium? There is something mysterious about a fish. How can it glide along so silently? How does it breathe under the water? What does it think about all day long?

The salmon is perhaps even more mysterious than most fish. It begins life in fresh water in a river or stream. As a "teenager," it travels downstream to the salty ocean. When the salmon's life is almost over, it fights its way back upstream to the same river or stream where it was born.

Why does the salmon travel so far? What does it do while at sea? How does it find its way back to the river or stream where it was born?

Questions like these have puzzled people for thousands of years. Long ago, storytellers used to say that salmon were really human beings.

These old stories said that the salmon people were princes and princesses. They had beautiful palaces in the depths of the ocean where they lived while they were at sea. When they wanted to come back inland, they put on robes of salmon flesh and swam up the rivers and streams.

Of course, we know today that these stories are not true. However, there is still an air of mystery about the remarkable salmon.

Sleek, slim and beautiful are just a few ways to describe the salmon-- mysterious too!

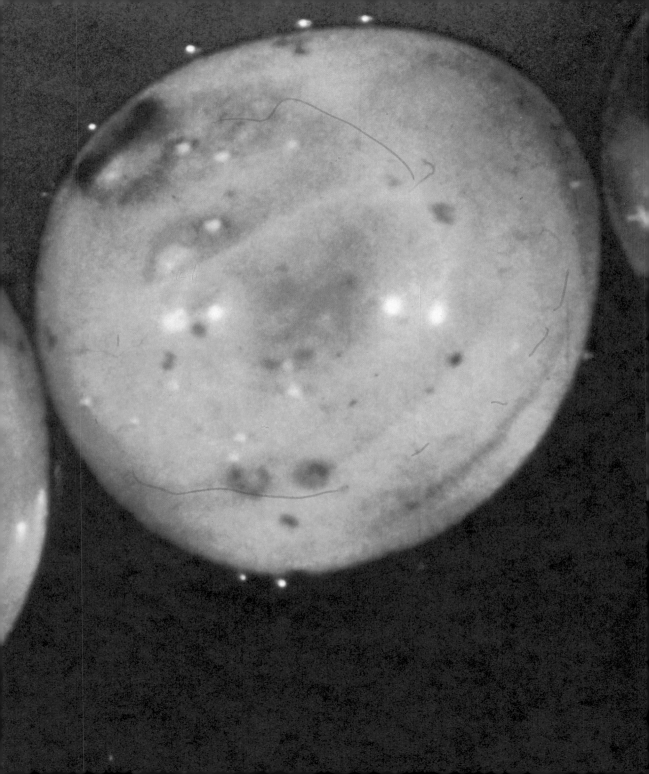

Tiny Pink Eggs

The salmon starts life as a round pink egg no bigger than a pea. The egg lies deep in the gravel under a swift-flowing river or stream. With it are hundreds of other little pink eggs. These will hatch to become the baby salmon's sisters and brothers.

The mother and father salmon will not be there when the eggs hatch. They do not really take care of their young in any way. However, the mother salmon hides her eggs in as safe a place as possible. She covers them with a deep layer of gravel, so that they are out of sight, but still surrounded by flowing water.

A few weeks later, two tiny black specks appear inside each pink egg. These are the eyes of the little creature growing inside.

Salmon eggs magnified to about 40 times their actual size.

Babies with "See-Through" Bodies

Soon the tiny fish begin to struggle inside their rubbery pink shells. This usually happens in late winter or spring. One by one, they break through their shells. Some come out head first, others tail first.

At this stage the baby salmon are called alevins. They have soft, see-through bodies. If you were to look at one, you could see straight through to its ribs and backbone. You would see the tiny heart just behind its mouth, busily pumping red blood.

The little alevin would seem to be staring right back at you. At this stage the baby salmon's eyes are enormous compared with its body.

On the underside of each alevin's body, you would see a round, hanging sac. This is the yolk sac from the alevin's egg. During the first few weeks after hatching, the baby salmon does not eat. Instead, it draws its nourishment from its yolk sac.

Opposite page:

The wide-eyed little alevin never has to worry about where its next meal will come from.

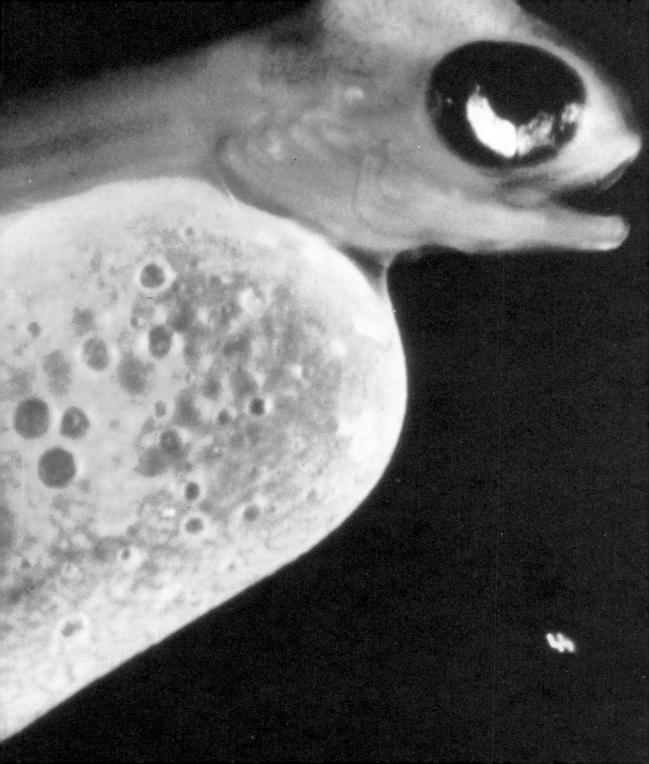

Egg

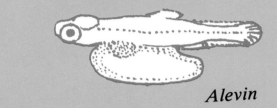

Alevin

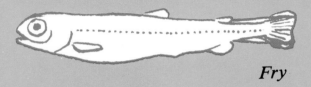

Fry

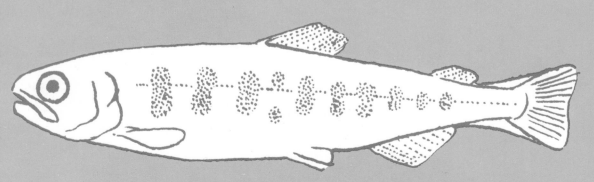

Adult

Small Fry

After several weeks, the alevins grow restless down in the gravel of their river or stream bed. Little by little they begin to wriggle up toward open water.

As time passes, the alevins' yolk sacs become smaller and smaller. At last the sacs disappear altogether. They have been completely taken up into the bodies of the baby salmon.

Once the baby salmon lose their yolk sacs, they are no longer alevins. They are now known as fry or parr. (Have you ever heard people speak of children as "small fry"? Now you know where this expression comes from!)

Like Real Fish at Last

The salmon fry, although only about two and a half centimetres (one inch) long, look much more like fish now. Tiny scales cover their bodies, and they have small, separate fins.

At first the fry eat any bits of food that happen to drift into their mouths. But soon they learn to go after food themselves. They start off eating the small larvae (hatched eggs) of insects. Gradually, they eat larger larvae and adult insects that fall into the pond. The salmon are strong, quick hunters. They soon learn to leap high out of the water after their prey.

The salmon fry do not only pursue prey. They are also pursued. Trout, perch and many other fish like to gobble up the tasty salmon fry. So do otters, eels and fish-eating birds such as kingfishers.

It's hard to believe that this tiny fish will one day weigh as much as a medium-sized dog.

Down to the Sea

Someday you will become a teenager. During your teen years, many changes will take place in your body. You will change from being a child to being an adult.

The life of the salmon is the same in a way. But the salmon reaches its "teenage" stage at only two to four years of age! Then major changes start taking place in the young fish's body. These changes prepare it to live in the adult world of the salmon—the ocean.

Soon after the changes begin, the young salmon leaves the stream or river where it hatched. It swims downstream toward the ocean along with others of its own kind. Sometimes the journey is as long as 3000 kilometres (1800 miles).

At last the young salmon reach a bay where their stream or river meets the ocean. There they linger for a while, almost as if they are deciding whether to go on or not. Finally, they strike out into the open ocean, where they will spend most of their adult lives.

Fresh Water, Salty Water

If you have ever gone swimming in the ocean, the taste of the water and the slight sting in your eyes may have told you that ocean water is salty.

Unlike ocean water, river and stream water is not salty. We call it fresh water. Some kinds of fish, such as trout, can live only in fresh water.

Some other kinds of fish, such as cod, can live only in salty water. If they swam into fresh water, they would soon die.

The salmon, however, is special. It is one of the few kinds of fish in the world that can live in both fresh and salty water. It is able to do so by increasing or decreasing the amount of salt in its body. The amount of salt changes to balance the amount of salt in the water.

Home, sweet, salmon home.

Cold-water Cousins

There are two main kinds of salmon in the world—Atlantic Salmon and Pacific Salmon. We call them cousins because they all belong to one big family of fish—the *Salmonidae* family.

Both of these salmon live in the northern third of the world. Why? Salmon like to live in cool or cold water. If you went swimming in water at the temperature that salmon like, you would soon start shivering. Salmon like water that is below about 14° C (57° F).

The more the merrier. Salmon, like most fish, often swim in a group called a school.

Comparative size of 5 types of Pacific Salmon

Pink

Chum

Coho

Sockeye

Chinook

Atlantic Salmon

Baby Atlantic Salmon hatch in the streams and rivers of Canada's Maritime provinces and Quebec and in those of the northeastern United States. Many Atlantic Salmon also hatch in the streams and rivers of Europe.

When young Atlantic Salmon reach the "teenage" stage, they make their way down to the Atlantic Ocean. Once out in the ocean, many swim far north to Arctic waters.

Pacific Salmon

Pacific Salmon found in North America are divided into five main groups: 1) sockeye 2) chum 3) pink 4) coho 5) chinook. They hatch in the cool streams and swift-flowing rivers of British Columbia and the western United States, down as far as northern California. Some Pacific Salmon are also born in Japan and Siberia.

When young Pacific Salmon reach the "teenage" stage, they make their way down to the Pacific Ocean. Once at sea, many swim far out into the northern Pacific to feed.

Opposite page:

Two salmon passing in the sea.

Meet the Full-grown Salmon

Like many other fish, the salmon has a long streamlined body that helps it glide through the water easily.

Salmon fins

Also, like most fish, it is covered with shiny scales that overlap like shingles on a roof. These scales are like a coat of armor. They help protect the fish from injury. Over its scales the salmon has a slimy-feeling coat of mucus. This too protects the salmon by helping it slip over rocks easily so that its scales are not hurt.

The salmon, like most fish, has several fins to help it swim. Its large V-shaped tail fin acts as a paddle and a rudder. On its belly the salmon has two smaller pairs of fins to help it turn and stop in the water. These small fins also help the salmon hover in the water while feeding. Behind these is a single fin that acts as a keel, holding the salmon upright in the water. The big fin sticking up on the salmon's back acts as a keel too. And the salmon can use the sharp spines on this fin to defend itself from attack by a predator.

Many Sizes, All Cleverly Disguised

Full-grown salmon vary a great deal in size, depending on the kind. Some kinds of salmon are full-grown at one kilogram (2.2 pounds). Others can weigh as much as 55 kilograms (120 pounds). An average full-grown salmon weighs about 13 kilograms (29 pounds) and is about 100 centimetres (40 inches) long. This makes it about as big as a medium-sized dog.

There are many different colors of salmon, but most have dark spots on their sides and backs and silvery colored bellies. There is a very good reason for this two-tone coloring. Seen from above, the salmon's dark spotted back helps it blend in against the rocks and weeds at the bottom. From below the salmon's silvery belly is hard to see against the bright water surface. What a clever disguise to fool predators!

That flash of silver on the salmon's belly not only looks pretty, but it's a useful disguise too.

Breathing Under Water

You breathe because you need oxygen from the air to stay alive. The salmon needs oxygen too. However, it cannot get this oxygen by breathing air as you do. Instead, the salmon gets its oxygen from water.

How a salmon breathes through its gills.

To do this, the fish uses its gills. Rounded, flap-like covers protect the gills. You may have noticed the gill covers on a salmon or other fish. They are on the sides of the fish's head, behind the mouth and eyes.

Underneath the gill covers, the salmon's gills are fleshy and bright red. The red color comes from the many small blood vessels in the gills.

As water passes over the salmon's gills, red blood cells in the blood vessels pick up oxygen. The salmon's bloodstream then carries the oxygen through its body. This keeps the fish alive and healthy.

Glubba, glubba, glub glub--Like all fish, a salmon breathes through gills--special slits at the sides of its head.

Krill

Let's Eat

A pink mass of wriggling creatures covers the ocean surface above a school (group) of salmon. Within the mass, each tiny shining body is rimmed with pink-orange light.

The salmon twist their solid powerful bodies and shoot up toward the surface. Jaws wide open, they hurl themselves at the pink mass, eating as fast as they can. At last all the crisp little pink creatures are gone. Their bellies full, the salmon lazily glide away.

A few hours later, however, the salmon will be hungry again. They will have to look for more food. Perhaps this time they will catch larger, livelier prey such as herring, smelt, small squid or eels. Or if they are lucky, they might come upon another squirming mass of "pink food."

The salmon's "pink food" is made up of shiny shrimplike creatures called krill. During their saltwater years, salmon eat large numbers of krill, as well as true shrimp. It is this diet of pink food that gives the salmon's flesh its pink color.

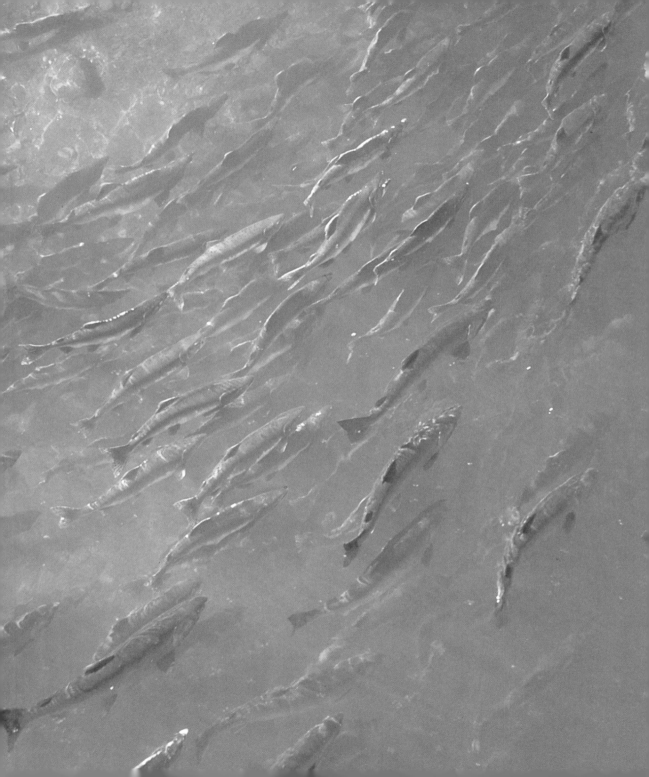

A Dangerous Life

All its life, the salmon must struggle hard to escape predators who would like nothing better than a meal of delicious pink salmon flesh.

Keen-eyed birds such as eagles, Herring Gulls, and cormorants prey upon the ocean-going salmon. Ocean mammals such as seals, Sea Lions, Killer Whales and porpoises also catch and eat salmon. So do sharks and some of the bigger fish, such as cod and tuna. Sometimes, the larger salmon will prey upon smaller salmon.

In many ways, the salmon is still a mystery to people. We really do not know how it thinks or how much it acts on instinct. One thing is certain. Any thinking that the salmon does probably centers on two subjects: how to get enough to eat, and how to avoid being eaten itself!

Finding the Way Home

After two, three or more years at sea, adult salmon leave the ocean and return to fresh water. They head straight for the inland rivers and streams where they were born. How do they know their way?

This question is part of the mystery of the salmon. We do not know the full answer. However, many scientists believe that salmon find their way to the coast by sensing the earth's magnetic field and the ocean's currents. Once they reach the coast their strong sense of smell helps to guide them. Each river has its own special smell, a mixture of all the odors of food, soil, weeds and rocks that are in the water. The salmon detects this smell and follows it home.

It's hard to miss a Pacific Salmon that's returning to spawn. That's because it's body is bright red and its head is grayish-green.

Up from the Sea

Thousands of pink eggs are now growing inside the female salmon's body. The egg mass bulges out on both sides of her body, making her look fat.

The male salmon, on the other hand, becomes thin and fierce looking. His eyes sink far into his head, and his upper jaw hooks down over his lower one. Sperm are ripening in his body. He will use these to fertilize a female's eggs.

From the time the salmon enter fresh water, they stop eating. They do not feel hungry any more. Their bodies live off the fat built up during years of ocean feeding.

Yet the salmon remain strong swimmers. They must be strong to battle their way upstream to their home river or stream. For weeks the salmon struggle against the current. Sometimes churning rapids and waterfalls loom up in their way. The salmon leap high into the air to clear them.

Opposite page:

Not even a waterfall will stop a determined salmon from reaching its spawning ground.

Home at Last

At last the salmon are home. They glide in and out among the same rocks where they swam as "small fry." They rest in the shade of the same trees that leaned out from shore and shaded them when they were young.

The salmon have returned home to spawn. Soon the female salmon begin to search in the gravel at the bottom for good places to dig their nests. Some even fight with each other. The largest and strongest females claim the best nesting areas.

Having chosen her spot, the female rolls over onto her side. She flutters her tail in the gravel of the stream bed, digging a hollow. She rests for a moment and then turns on her side to begin digging again.

Here's a stream that's bursting with life. All these salmon are swimming home to spawn.

New Life

A male salmon swims up beside her. Another follows, also anxious to mate with the female. However, the fierce looking first male charges at the second male and drives him away.

By now the female has used her powerful fluttering tail to make her hollow about half a metre (over a foot and a half) deep. She hovers over it. Hundreds of tiny pale-pink eggs stream from her body.

At that same moment the male salmon, close beside the female, sends out a milky stream of fluid containing his sperm.

The sperm fertilize the eggs, joining with them to start new life growing. It is from the combined eggs and sperm that baby salmon will hatch.

Pacific Salmon moms lay between three and five thousand eggs.

Tired Salmon

What will protect the little eggs till they hatch? The mother salmon takes care of that. She swims upstream and begins to dig a new hollow. Some of the gravel from this new hollow drifts down and covers the fertilized eggs in the first nest.

The mother salmon keeps digging gravel nests and laying her eggs. She may repeat the process up to eight times. Each time the male is right beside her, fertilizing the eggs as she lays them.

At last the female has no more eggs. Both she and the male are tired out. So are the other salmon who have been spawning in the stream.

No longer able to swim against the current, the tired fish begin to drift downstream. They are skinny and sick looking. Their fins are ragged. Their scales are falling off. The withered brown leaves of autumn fall around them. Insects shimmer on the surface of the water. But the weary salmon hardly notice. At last they die.

Opposite page:

Many Atlantic Salmon return to the sea after they spawn.

Life Goes On

Most salmon die after spawning only once. All Pacific Salmon do so. However, some Atlantic Salmon actually live to return to sea. After several years at sea, these "second lifers" come back home to spawn a second time. A few have been known to spawn three or more times.

But this is rare. For most salmon, life is over after one spawning.

This seems sad . . . until we remember the thousands of tiny pink eggs buried in the gravel beneath the rivers and streams. Soon new life inside them will be stirring. Then the story of the salmon will start all over again.

Words to Know

Alevin   A newly hatched salmon, still with its yolk sac attached.

Blood cells   Tiny solid particles in blood, some of which (the red cells) carry oxygen to all parts of the body.

Fins   Parts of a fish's body which the fish uses to balance, propel and steer itself.

Fry   A young salmon after it has used up its yolk sac. Sometimes also called parr.

Gills   Openings in a fish's body that take in oxygen.

Krill   Tiny pink shrimplike creatures that make up most of the adult salmon's diet.

Larvae   The second stage of an insect's life which occurs after it has hatched from the egg.

Predator   An animal that hunts other fish or animals for food.

Prey   An animal that is hunted for food.

Spawn   To deposit eggs.

Sperm   A substance produced by the male to fertilize the eggs.

INDEX

Cover Photo: G. Van Rijckevorsel (Valan Photos)

Photo Credits: G. Van Rijckevorsel (Valan Photos), pages 4, 6, 16, 20, 29, 35, 44; Nova Scotia Department of Fisheries and Oceans, pages 8, 11; Atlantic Salmon Federation, pages 15, 30; Tim Fitzharris (First Light Associated Photographers), page 19; Thomas Kitchin (Valan Photos), page 22; Wilf Schurig (Valan Photos), page 26; H. Armstrong Roberts (Miller Services), pages 33, 39; Dennis W. Schmidt (Valan Photos), pages 36, 40, 43.